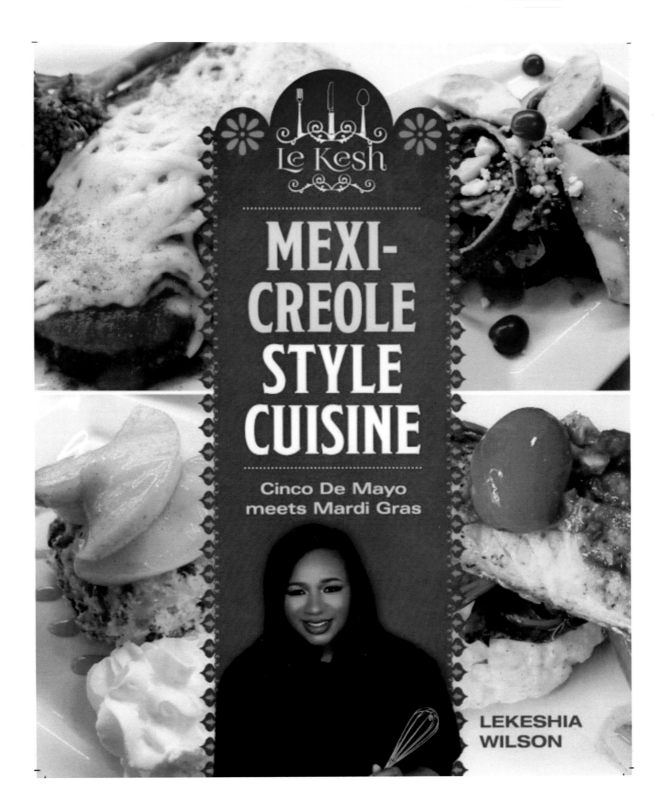

Le Kesh

MEXI-CREOLE STYLE CUISINE

Cinco De Mayo meets Mardi Gras

LEKESHIA WILSON

Mexi-Creole Style Cuisine
Copyright © 2020 Lekeshia Wilson

ISBN: 978-0-578-70195-0

Printed by Steuben Press.

First printing, 2020.

www.Lekesh.com

This book is dedicated to my mother, Loistene White. She embodies the meaning of hard work, sacrifice, and loving unconditionally, effortlessly. Her strong faith taught me the power of God, who delivered me out of the toughest times and is the source of my blessings that are so abundant.

Table of Contents

This is How "WE" BRUNCH

Everyday is "Fat Tuesday" ENTREES

Pass Me the Sauce MISCELLANEOUS

Let's "Mardi Gras Parade" to these DESSERTS

This is How "WE" BRUNCH

My favorite moments always seem to involve a gathering that includes food. One of my favorite brunch memories was our 1ˢᵗ annual Wilson Mother's Day Celebration in 2019. Our busy schedules always seem to collide with everyone graduating from college and moving from state-to-state. Finally, we found the time to reconnect. And oh, it was worth it! That weekend created lasting memories for us all.

Make time to make memories….God, then Family!

Crab & Shrimp Fondeaux
with Cheese Texas Toast

PREP: 10 MIN	TOTAL: 30 MIN	4 SERVINGS

What to Buy

Jumbo Shrimp · Mushrooms · Green Onions · Spinach · Broth · Butter · White Wine · Salt

Lump Crab · Shallots · Whole Garlic · Bay Leaf · Heavy Cream · Parmesan & Mozzarella Cheese · LeKesh Blackened

Pairing Suggestion

Our favorite pairing with this dish is a Vodka Tonic Martini.

Utensils

- 2 Large Skillets
- Measuring Spoons
- Ovenproof pan
- Measuring Cups
- Cooking Spoon
- Knife
- Cutting Board

Ingredients

- 12 raw jumbo shrimp, peeled and deveined, cut into 3 pieces
- ½ cup lump crab meat
- 3 tablespoons butter, divided
- 1 shallot, minced
- 4 cloves garlic, minced
- ¼ cup white wine
- 2 cup heavy cream
- ½ cup vegetable broth
- 1 teaspoon LeKesh Blackened seasoning or store bought
- 1/4 teaspoon salt
- 1 cup fresh spinach, chopped
- 4 oz. mushrooms, sliced
- 3 stalks of green onions, chopped
- 2 cups mozzarella cheese shredded
- 1 cup parmesan shredded

Crab & Shrimp Fondeaux
with Cheese Texas Toast

1 PREPARE

Wash and dry all of the vegetables. Next, mince the shallots, mince garlic cloves, chop green onions, and chop the spinach.

In a large skillet, combine 2 tablespoons of butter, shallot, and garlic. Cook over medium heat until shallots are tender, about 2 minutes. Slowly stir in the white wine until nearly absorbed (about 1 minutes), then incorporate the parmesan. Whisk in the cream and vegetable broth. Add, salt and bay leaves, then simmer for 5 more minutes. Remove from heat and set aside.

2 SEASON THE SHRIMP

Season shrimp with LeKesh Blackened seasoning.

3 SAUTE SHRIMP & VEGGIES

In another skillet, melt 1 tablespoon butter over medium heat. Sauté shrimp in butter about 2 minutes per side. Add spinach, mushrooms, crab meat, green onions, and salt. Sauté until mushrooms and spinach have softened, about 2 minutes. Fold the vegetable mixture into cream sauce and bring to a simmer. Remove the bay leaves. Add the mozzarella. Simmer another 2 minutes until the cheese is melted.

4 BROIL IN THE OVEN

Pour the mixture into an ovenproof dish. Top with parmesan cheese. Place under a broiler until cheese melts and is golden brown, about 5 minutes.

5 PLATE & SERVE

Garnish with chives (optional). Serve immediately with crostini or cheesy garlic bread (Texas Toast). ENJOY!

Crawfish Étouffée Omelet

PREP: 10 MIN	TOTAL: 40 MIN	4 SERVINGS

What to Buy

Crawfish Tails   Diced Tomatoes   Flour   Butter   Green Pepper   Green Onions   Mexican Cheese   Salt

Eggs   Yellow Onions   Whole Garlic   Parsley   Bay Leaves   Olive Oil   LeKesh Cajun   Heavy Whipping Cream

Pairing Suggestion

Our favorite pairing with this meal is Chardonnay.

Utensils

- 2 Large Skillets
- Cooking Spoon
- Knife
- Cutting Board
- Mixing Bowl
- Measuring Spoons
- Measuring Cups
- Cheese Grater

Ingredients

- 2 pounds crawfish tail meat
- 1 stick salted butter
- 1 large onion, diced
- 1/2 bell pepper, seeded and diced
- 6 cloves garlic, minced
- 3 fresh bay leaves
- ½ cup all-purpose flour
- 1 cup diced canned tomatoes
- 1 teaspoon salt
- 1 tablespoon LeKesh Cajun
- 1/2 cup chopped green onion
- 2 tablespoons chopped parsley
- 4 tablespoons olive oil
- 8 eggs
- 1 cup Mexican Cheese
- ¼ cup heavy whipping cream

Crawfish Étouffée Omelet

1 PREPARE

Wash and dry all of the vegetables. Next, dice the onions and bell peppers, mince garlic cloves, chop the parsley and green onions; placing each in a separate bowl or separate on the chopping board in different sections.

2 SAUTE THE VEGETABLES

Heat the butter in a large skillet over medium heat. Add the onions, peppers, and garlic. Cook for 8 minutes or until the vegetables well sautéed and translucent in color.

3 CREATE THE ROUX

Add the flour slowly, stirring to ensure flour doesn't get stuck to the bottom of the skillet. Cook for about 5 minutes, then add the tomatoes, LeKesh Cajun seasoning, and bay leaves, then cook another 3 minutes.

4 ADD CRAWFISH

Add the crawfish tails and parsley. Stirring occasionally, cook for about 10 minutes. Remove the bay leaves.

5 CREATE 4 OMELETES

In a mixing bowl, combine the eggs with heavy whipping cream. Heat another skillet to medium, add 1 tablespoon olive oil to the skillet. You will divide mixture into approximately 4 for four omelets, pouring the mixture into the skillet each time. Allow the egg to solidify 1-2 minutes, then fold. Cook 2 more minutes, then top with Mexican cheese.

6 PLATE & SERVE

Plate an omelet onto each plate, then spoon desired amount of crawfish mixture over each, then garnish with green onions.

Creole Crab Quiche

PREP: 10 MIN	TOTAL: 40 MIN	4 SERVINGS

What to Buy

Lump Crab • Heavy Whipping Cream • Lemons • Butter • Mexican Cheese • Deep Dish Pie Crust

Eggs • Shallots • Whole Garlic • Fresh Parsley • Parm, Asiago, Romano • LeKesh Cajun

Pairing Suggestion

Our favorite pairing with this meal is New Zealand Sauvignon Blanc.

Utensils

- Large Skillet
- Cooking Spoon
- Knife
- Cutting Board
- Whisk
- Mixing Bowl
- Measuring Spoons
- Measuring Cups
- Cheese Grater

Ingredients

- 2 cups lump crab
- ¾ cup parmesan, asiago, romano shredded cheese
- ¼ cup shredded Mexican Cheese
- 2 deep shell pie shells
- 2 cups heavy whipping cream
- 1 shallot, minced
- 4 garlic cloves, minced
- 2 tablespoons butter
- 2 fresh parsley, chopped
- Zest of 1 lemon
- 4 eggs, beaten
- 1 tablespoons LeKesh Cajun seasoning

Creole Crab Quiche

 1 PREPARE

Preheat Oven to 350.

Mince the shallots, chop the parsley, and minced garlic. Next, zest the lemon using a cheese grater.

 2 CREATE THE FILLING

Melt butter in a large skillet over medium heat, then add the shallots and minced garlic. Add the cheeses, then stir until melted (1-2 minutes) lowering the heat to low. Add LeKesh Cajun seasoning, then whisk in the heavy whipping cream and eggs. Turn off the heat.

 3 FILL THE SHELLS

Fill each of the pie shells with lump crab, spreading evenly across the bottom. Sprinkle parsley across the top of crab, then fill each shell evenly with liquid cheese mixture.

 4 BAKE THE QUICHE

Place pies in oven for 25-30 minutes until center of pie is set. Once done, sprinkle with remaining parsley and cool for 10 minutes.

 5 PLATE & SERVE

Slice the quiche and place onto individual plates. ENJOY!

Note: The extra cooked pie can be placed into an oven bag then frozen for later use. When ready to reheat, bake 25-30 minutes in the oven.

Fried Lobster & Cheddar Herb Waffles
with Spicy Honey Butter

PREP: 10 MIN	TOTAL: 45 MIN	4 SERVINGS

What to Buy

Lobster Tails · Milk · Seafood Breading · Sugar · Lemons · Shredded Cheddar · Butter · Honey · Crushed Red Pepper · Salt

All-Purpose Flour · Baking Powder · Buttermilk · Pure Vanilla Extract · Eggs · Fresh Chives · Vegetable Oil · LeKesh Cajun

Pairing Suggestion

Our favorite pairing with this meal is a Moscow Mule.

Utensils

- Waffle Iron

- Whisk

- Cooking Spoon

- Kitchen Shears

- Cutting Board

- 4 Mixing Bowls

- Frying Pan

- Measuring Spoons

- Measuring Cups

Ingredients

- 2 jumbo lobster tails
- 2 cups all-purpose flour
- ½ teaspoon salt
- 1 tablespoon baking powder
- 1/4 cup sugar
- 1 ½ cup milk
- 2 ½ tablespoons pure vanilla extract
- 4 egg whites, 2 egg yolks
- 2 sticks butter, divided
- ½ cup shredded cheddar
- ½ cup honey
- 1/2 tablespoon red pepper flakes
- 3 tablespoons fresh chives, chopped
- 1 tablespoon LeKesh Cajun
- 1 ½ cup favorite seafood breading
- 1 cup buttermilk
- Zest of 1 lemon
- 3 cups vegetable oil

Fried Lobster & Cheddar Herb Waffles

1 ## PREPARE WAFFLE

For the waffle: In one mixing bowl combine flour, sugar, salt, baking powder using a whisk or sifter.

In another mixing bowl, combine the egg yolks, vanilla extract, and milk. Melt 1 stick butter whisk into mixture. Fold into dry mixture.

Whisk or beat the egg whites under they become thick in texture, almost stiff, then combine with mixture. Stir in Cheddar & ½ of the chives.

2 ## GRILL THE WAFFLE

Heat the waffle iron. Scoop ¾ cup mixture onto waffle iron and grill until crisp. Complete in batches until all of the batter has been used. Place waffles on individual plates.

3 ## PREPARE LOBSTER

For the Fried Lobster: Wash the lobster tails and pat them dry with a paper towel. Using kitchen shears, cut through the shell down the middle, pull the meat out, then slice the tails half lengthwise. Season the lobster with LeKesh Cajun season.

Take one mixing bowl and pour in your seafood breading. In another bowl, pour the buttermilk.

Cover the lobster in seafood batter, then dip in buttermilk, and repeat the steps until all lobster is battered.

4 ## DEEP FRY THE LOBSTER

Heat the oil in pot over medium heat. Once hot, place lobster tail in oil and fry for 3-4 minutes until golden. Remove from heat.

5 ## PLATE & SERVE

Place the lobster over the waffles. Garnish with chives. Serve with warm syrup and Spicy Honey Butter (Melted Butter, Red Pepper, Honey blended). ENJOY!

Apple Cinnamon French Toast
Topped with Buttercream Frosting

PREP: 10 MIN	TOTAL: 30 MIN	4 SERVINGS

What to Buy

Apples	Pure Vanilla Flavor	Lemons	Honey Wheat Bread	Butter	Powdered Sugar
Eggs	Cinnamon	All-Spice	Sugar	Powdered Sugar	Heavy Whipping Cream

Pairing Suggestion

Our favorite pairing with this meal is an Aperol Spritz.

Utensils

- 2 Large Skillets

- Cooking Spoon

- Knife

- Cutting Board

- 2 Mixing Bowls

- Measuring Spoons

- Measuring Cups

- Whisk

- Hand Mixer

Ingredients

CINNAMON APPLES

- 3 red apples, thinly sliced
- 2 tablespoons cinnamon
- 1 teaspoon all-spice
- 1 cup brown sugar
- 1 cup sugar`
- 1 stick butter
- Juice of 1 lemon

FRENCH TOAST

- 4 eggs
- ¼ cup heavy whipping cream
- 8 slices honey wheat bread

BUTTERCREAM

- 2 tablespoons vanilla extract
- 3 cups powder sugar (confectioners)
- 1 cup butter
- 1 teaspoon vanilla extract
- 1 to 2 tablespoons whipping cream

Apple Cinnamon French Toast
Topped with Buttercream Frosting

 1 ## PREPARE

Peel the apples, then slice thinly and squeeze lemon juice on top to cover, then place to the side.

Take out mixing bowls and in each bowl, combine: 2 tablespoons cinnamon, 1 teaspoon all-spice, 1 cup sugar, and 1 cup brown sugar. Mix well then toss in the apple mixture and place the bowl to the side.

In a third bowl, using a fork, mix the eggs with heavy whipping cream. Mix the dry mixture into the egg mixture and combine well using a whisk.

 2 ## DIP THE BREAD

Heat one of the skillets to medium with 1 tablespoon of butter. Then, dip each side of bread into the egg mixture ensuring fully covered and dripping off any excess liquid. Then place the bread into the hot skillet until well toasted on each side (about 2 minutes). Put each French toast on a lined plate when complete. Repeat steps until all the bread is complete.

3 ## SAUTÉ THE APPLES

Heat the other skillet to medium with ½ stick of butter. Pour the apple mixture in, lower heat cook for 10 minutes until softened.

 4 ## PREPARE BUTTERCREAM

With a hand or standing mixer, blend together the sugar and butter on low speed. Add in the vanilla and cream until well mixed, increase the speed and mix for an additional 2 minutes.

 5 ## PLATE & SERVE

On each individual plate, place desired number of French Toast, top with Apple Cinnamon Compote, then drizzle with Buttercream Frosting. ENJOY!

Tomato & Mozzarella Omelet Sandwich

with Pesto Sauce

PREP: 5 MIN	TOTAL: 10 MIN	1 SERVINGS

What to Buy

Egg	Butter	Honey Wheat Bread	Basil Leaves	Salt
Sun-dried Tomatoes	Mozzarella	Pesto Sauce	Olive Oil	Black Pepper

Pairing Suggestion

Our favorite pairing with this meal is a Tequila Sunrise.

Utensils

- 2 Large Skillets
- Measuring Spoons

- Cooking Spoon
- Cutting Board

- Knife

Ingredients

- 1 slice fresh mozzarella cheese
- 1 egg
- 4 basil leaves, torn in half
- 2 tablespoons sun-dried tomatoes
- 1 tablespoon pesto sauce
- 2 slices of honey wheat bread
- Drizzle olive oil
- 1 tablespoon butter
- Salt
- Pepper

Tomato & Mozzarella Omelet Sandwich
with Pesto Sauce

 1 PREPARE

Place each bread slice into a plate. Spread pesto on one side, then top with basil leaves. On the other side, spread the sun-dried tomatoes. Top the tomatoes with the mozzarella slice.

 2 SCRAMBLE THE EGG

In one of the skillets, drizzle enough olive oil to coat the pan. Pour your scrambled egg into the skillet and let it sit until the egg becomes firm enough to fold into an omelet. Season with salt and pepper. Then place the omelet onto bread and close the bread together.

 3 GRILL

In the other skillet, melt the butter, then toast both sides of the sandwich to your liking. Remove from heat.

4 PLATE & SERVE

Place onto a plate. ENJOY!

Grilled Shrimp Verde Bowl

PREP: 10 MIN	TOTAL: 40 MIN	4 SERVINGS

What to Buy

Jumbo Shrimp	Jasmine Rice	Poblano Pepper	Black Beans	LeKesh Creamy Verde	Mexican Cheese	Salsa	Limes
Jalapenos or Serrano's	White Onions	Whole Garlic	Fresh Cilantro	Olive Oil	LeKesh Mexican		

Pairing Suggestion

Our favorite pairing with this meal is a Mexican Lager Beer.

Utensils

- Large Skillet
- Pot
- Cooking Spoon
- Mixing Bowl
- Knife
- Measuring Spoons
- Cutting Board
- Measuring Cups
- Cheese Grater

Ingredients

- 2 pounds raw jumbo shrimp
- 4 tablespoons olive oil, plus a drizzle
- 3 tablespoons + ½ tablespoon LeKesh Mexican Seasoning or taco seasoning of choice
- 1 cup of Mexican or Chihuahua Cheese
- 1 ½ cups jasmine rice
- Juice and zest of ½ lime
- 2 tablespoons cilantro, minced
- 1 poblano pepper, diced
- 2 garlic cloves, minced
- 1 jalapeno or serrano pepper, sliced
- ½ white onion, minced
- 1 can of black beans
- LeKesh Creamy Salsa Verde (see recipe)
- Jar of salsa

Grilled Shrimp Verde Bowl

1 PREPARE

Mince the garlic, jalapenos, white onion, juice and zest the lime, then dice the poblano pepper. Set aside.

2 BOIL THE RICE

Turn heat to medium-high. Drizzle olive oil in a pot. Next pour in the jasmine rice, minced cilantro, lime juice and zest, and 2 ¼ cups water. Once water begins to boil, reduce heat to low and simmer covering pot with a lid. Be sure not to stir rice, let cook 15-18 minutes undisturbed.

3 SAUTÉ THE VEGGIES

Heat 1 tablespoon of olive oil in a skillet over medium heat. Add the poblano and onions. Sauté the vegetables until translucent. Then stir in black beans and season with 11/2 tablespoon LeKesh Mexican

4 COOK THE SHRIMP

Season the shrimp with 2 tablespoons of LeKesh Mexican season. Heat 1 tablespoon of olive oil in another skillet over medium heat. Add shrimp to the skillet in batches. Cook the shrimp for 3 minutes on each side. Set shrimp to the side.

5 PLATE & SERVE

In individual bowls, scoop rice, then poblano bean mixture, then shrimp, then top with salsa, creamy verde salsa, and regular salsa. Garnish with jalapeno slices and sprinkle with Mexican seasoning.

Mexican Street Corn

Also Known As, "Elote"

PREP: 10 MIN	TOTAL: 30 MIN	4 SERVINGS

What to Buy

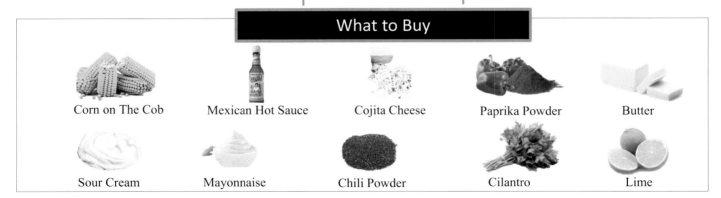

Corn on The Cob	Mexican Hot Sauce	Cojita Cheese	Paprika Powder	Butter
Sour Cream	Mayonnaise	Chili Powder	Cilantro	Lime

Pairing Suggestion

Our favorite pairing with this meal is a Tequila Club Soda Martini with sweetened lime juice.

Utensils

- Large Skillet

- Roasting Pan

- Cooking Spoon

- Knife

- Whisk

- Measuring Spoons

- Measuring Cups

- Cutting Board

- Mixing Bowl

Ingredients

- 4 ears sweet corn on the cob husks pulled back and silks removed or corn off the cob
- 4 tablespoons of cold butter
- 1 teaspoon of chili powder
- ¼ cup of sour cream
- ¼ cup of mayonnaise
- 1 tablespoon fresh cilantro
- ½ cup of crumbled cotija cheese
- smoked paprika to taste
- Dashes of Mexican hot sauce (optional)
- 1 lime cut into wedges

Mexican Street Corn

Also Known As, "Elote"

1 **PREPARE**

Preheat grill or oven to 400 degrees.

2 **BUTTER THE CORN**

Rub ears of corn with cold butter (easier to coat the raw ears of corn evenly). Grill, bake, or boil corn until tender, turning a couple of times to char evenly.

**If using canned corn, place the contents in a skillet, then steam the corn 10 minutes over medium heat. Drain the excess liquid, then place the butter in the skillet and turn off heat.

3 **CREATE THE CHILI CREMA**

Meanwhile, in a small bowl whisk chili powder into the sour cream and mayonnaise, then set aside.

4 **ADD THE TOPPINGS**

Remove corn from grill, oven, or skillet, then spread each cob evenly with chili creama (for canned corn, mix in the chili creama). Top corn with cotija, cilantro, smoked paprika, and hot sauce (optional).

5 **PLATE & SERVE**

Place onto individual plates or small bowls. Serve with lime wedges. ENJOY!

Shrimp Quesadillas

with Creamy Salsa Verde & Homemade Guacamole

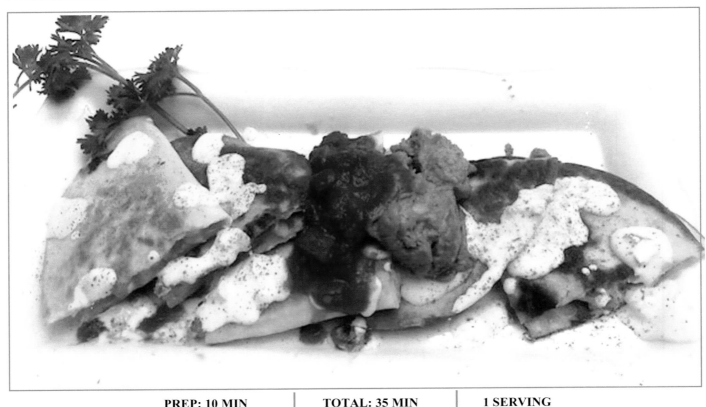

PREP: 10 MIN	TOTAL: 35 MIN	1 SERVING

What to Buy

Jumbo Shrimp	Flour Tortillas	Lime	Salsa	Jalapenos	Guacamole
Mexican Cheese	White Onion	Whole Garlic	Fresh Cilantro	Olive Oil	LeKesh Mexican

Pairing Suggestion

Our favorite pairing with this meal is a Traditional Lime Margarita.

Utensils

- Large Skillet

- Roasting Pan

- Cooking Spoon

- Knife

- Cutting Board

- Mixing Bowl

- Measuring Spoons

- Measuring Cups

- Cheese Grater

Ingredients

- 6 raw jumbo shrimp, peeled and deveined
- 2 tablespoons olive oil
- 2 tablespoons LeKesh Mexican Seasoning or taco seasoning of choice
- 1 cup of Mexican or Chihuahua Cheese
- 2 large flour tortillas
- 1 cup sour cream
- Juice of 1 lime
- Zest of 1 lime
- 2 garlic cloves, minced
- 1 jalapeno minced
- ½ white onion, minced
- LeKesh Guacamole (see recipe) or store bought
- Jar of salsa

Shrimp Quesadillas
with Salsa Verde & Homemade Guacamole

1 PREPARE

Mince the garlic, jalapenos, and white onion, then juice and zest the lime.

Preheat skillet on medium adding 2 tablespoons of olive oil to the pan.

2 COOK THE SHRIMP

Season shrimp with 1 tablespoon LeKesh Mexican seasoning. Add the shrimp to the skillet and cook undisturbed for 3 minutes on each side. Remove from pan, then chop into bit-sized pieces.

3 FILL & FOLD QUESADILLAS

Fill one side of each tortilla with 1/2 cup of cheese, then top with shrimp (splitting the portion between both tortillas). Using the remaining 1 tablespoon of LeKesh Mexican Seasoning, sprinkle a little more on mixture. Then fold each tortilla.

4 MAKE THE SALSA VERDE

In a mixing bowl combine: sour cream, juice of lime, zest of lime, garlic, minced jalapeños, minced white onions, cilantro, and 1 tablespoon LeKesh Mexican. Stir with a spoon until combined. Place in the refrigerator until needed.

5 PAN GRILL

Place the quesadillas in the skillet and grill 2-3 minutes on each side until golden brown. Cut into triangle wedges.

6 PLATE & SERVE

Place quesadilla onto individual plates, then top with creamy salsa verde, guacamole, and salsa. ENJOY!

Jerk Salmon Taco Salad
with LeKesh Signature Fixings

PREP: 10 MIN	TOTAL: 40 MIN	4 SERVINGS

What to Buy

Salmon	Taco Doritos	Spring Salad Mix	Olive Oil	LeKesh Mango Habanero Slaw	Jerk Sauce	Salt

White Cheddar	Avocados	Cilantro	LeKesh Mexican Corn	LeKesh Agave Mustard Dressing	Black Pepper

Pairing Suggestion

Our favorite pairing with this meal is a Mango Margarita.

Utensils

- Large Skillet

- Roasting Pan

- Cooking Spoon

- Knife

- Cutting Board

- Mixing Bowl

- Measuring Spoons

- Measuring Cups

Ingredients

- 4-4 oz. salmon fillets
- 2 tablespoons olive oil
- 8 tablespoons LeKesh Jerk Sauce (see recipe) or store bought
- Taco Doritos or any flavor
- 1 cup shredded white cheddar cheese
- 1 avocado, thinly sliced
- 4 cups spring salad mix
- 4 tablespoons cilantro, minced
- LeKesh Mexican Corn (page 20)
- LeKesh Mango Habanero Slaw (page 79)
- LeKesh Agave Honey Mustard (page 78)
- Salt
- Pepper

Jerk Salmon Taco Salad
with LeKesh Signature Fixings

 1 PREPARE

Preheat the oven to 375.

Wash and dry all of the vegetables. Next, mince the cilantro and slice the avocado. Then rinse the salmon and pat dry with a paper towel.

 2 SEAR THE SALMON

Heat the skillet with olive oil over medium heat. Season the salmon with salt and pepper, then add to heat; cooking 3 minutes on each side undisturbed. Remove from heat, then brush each salmon fillet with Jerk Sauce, making sure to cover both sides.

 3 BAKE THE SALMON

Place the salmon in the roasting pan and cook for another 15 minutes for medium and 20-25 medium well – well done.

 4 PREPARE THE FIXINGS

See the appropriate pages for the following recipes: LeKesh Mexican Corn, Mango Habanero Slaw, and Agave Honey Mustard.

 5 PLATE & SERVE

On each individual plate, place 1 cup of salad mix, 1 salmon fillet, ¼ cup cheese, a few of the avocado slices, a tablespoon of cilantro, a spoonful of Mexican corn, Habanero Slaw, and a handful of Doritos. Serve with LeKesh Agave Honey Mustard to the side. ENJOY!

Waldorf Salad
with Agave Honey Mustard

| PREP: 10 MIN | TOTAL: 25 MIN | 4 SERVINGS |

What to Buy

| Red Apples | Romaine Lettuce | Cashew | Apple Cider Vinegar | Cinnamon | Bleu Cheese | Salt |
| Grape | Red Onions | Celery | Agave | Honey Mustard | Olive Oil | LeKesh Blackened | Black Pepper |

Pairing Suggestion

Our favorite pairing with this salad is an Aperol Spritz.

Utensils

- 2 Mixing Bowls
- Cooking Spoon
- Knife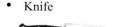
- Cutting Board
- Measuring Spoons
- Measuring Cups
- Whisk

Ingredients

- 1/2 cup crumbled blue cheese
- 1/4 cup red onion, diced
- 1/8 teaspoon ground black pepper
- 2 cups red apples, diced
- 1 cup celery, sliced thinly
- 1/2 cup red seedless grapes, halved
- 1/2 cup honey cashew pieces
- 1 head romaine lettuce

Agave Honey Mustard Dressing:

- 1/4 cup plus 1 tablespoon Dijon mustard
- 1/4 cup agave syrup
- 1/4 cup cider vinegar
- 1 1/2 teaspoons kosher salt
- 1 tablespoon parsley
- 1 teaspoon ground cinnamon
- 1/4 cup plus 2 tablespoons olive oil (may use soy, peanut, or corn)

Waldorf Salad
with Agave Honey Mustard

 1 PREPARE

Dice the red apples, thinly slice the celery, half the grapes, and chop the parsley. Place items to the side on a cutting board on individual mini bowls.

 2 TOSS THE SALAD

In a large bowl, combine the lettuce, apples, celery, grapes, red onions, blue cheese, black pepper, and cashews.

 3 BLEND THE DRESSING

In a mixing bowl, whisk the mustard, agave, vinegar, parsley, cinnamon, and salt. Gradually whisk in the olive oil to make a creamy dressing.

 4 PLATE & SERVE

Spoon salad on individual plates, drizzle with Agave Honey Mustard. ENJOY!

Smothered Potatoes

PREP: 10 MIN	TOTAL: 40 MIN	4 SERVINGS

What to Buy

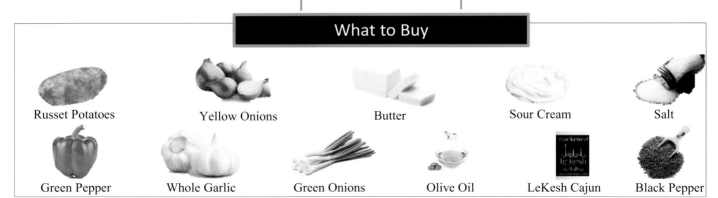

Russet Potatoes | Yellow Onions | Butter | Sour Cream | Salt

Green Pepper | Whole Garlic | Green Onions | Olive Oil | LeKesh Cajun | Black Pepper

Pairing Suggestion

Our favorite pairing with this meal is an Irish Cream Coffee.

Utensils

- Mixing Bowl
- Roasting Pan
- Knife
- Measuring Spoons
- Cooking Spoon
- Cutting Board

Ingredients

- 3 russet potatoes, diced with skin
- 1/2 yellow onion diced
- 1/4 green pepper, diced
- 2 garlic cloves minced
- 3 stalks green onions, separating green from white
- 2 tablespoons olive oil
- 2 tablespoons butter melted
- 1/2 tablespoon LeKesh Cajun
- 1/4 teaspoon salt
- 1/4 teaspoon pepper
- Sour cream (optional garnish)

Smothered Potatoes

 ## PREPARE

Preheat oven to 375.

Spray the bottom of a roasting pan with non-stick spray or spread a drizzle of olive oil.

 ## COMBINE MIXTURE

In a bowl mix the potatoes, onions, green pepper, garlic, and white potion of the green onions. Season the mix with LeKesh Cajun, salt, and pepper, then spread evenly across the pan. Drizzle the olive oil and butter across the potatoes.

 ## ROAST THE POTATOES

Roast the potatoes for 30 minutes or until the potato skin is crispy.

 ## PLATE & SERVE

Scoop onto individual plates or in bowls, then top with sour cream. Enjoy!

Everyday is "Fat Tuesday"
ENTREES

No one can deny that Chicago is a food city. Over the 13 years I lived there, my goal was to dine at the top 100 restaurants throughout the city. Little did I know, turnover of restaurants happened quickly; so my top favorites ended up closing and being replaced with a new favorite and the cycle continued. Throughout the Chicago journey, I always had a core group of friends who seemed to think that everyday was "Fat Tuesday."

Make time to make memories….with Friends!

Crawfish Pie

PREP: 10 MIN	TOTAL: 60 MIN	4 SERVINGS

What to Buy

Crawfish	Mushrooms	Bay Leaves	Butter	Green Onions	Pie Crust	Salt
Green Pepper	Yellow Onion	Whole Garlic	Fresh Parsley	Heavy Whipping Cream	LeKesh Cajun	

Pairing Suggestion

Our favorite pairing with this meal is a Rosé.

Utensils

- Large Skillet

- Deep Pie Pan

- Cooking Spoon

- Knife

- Measuring Spoons

- Measuring Cups

- Cutting Board

Ingredients

- 2 pounds crawfish tail meat
- 1/2 cup salted butter
- 1 large onion, diced (about 1 1/2 cups)
- 1/2 bell pepper, seeded and diced (about 1/2 cup)
- 6 cloves garlic, minced
- 1/2 cup mushrooms, chopped
- 3 Fresh bay leaves
- 1 pint heavy whipping cream
- 1 teaspoon salt
- 1 tablespoon LeKesh Cajun
- 1/2 cup, chopped green onion
- 2 tablespoon, chopped parsley
- 1 package ready-made pie crust (store bought)

Crawfish Pie

 1 PREPARE

Preheat oven to 400 degrees.

Wash and dry all of the vegetables. Next, dice the onions and bell pepper, mince the garlic, chop the mushrooms, parsley, and green onions; placing each in a separate bowl or separate on the chopping board in different sections.

 2 CREATE THE MIXTURE

In a large skillet, melt butter over medium heat; add onion, bell pepper, mushroom, and garlic; cook until softened. Add heavy whipping cream, LeKesh Cajun seasoning, and salt. Reduce heat to low, add bay leaves, and cook until thickened, about 5 minutes. Fold in crawfish, green onion, and parsley; cook 5 minutes. Remove bay leaves.

 3 BAKE & FILL THE CRUST

Firmly press the bottom crust into a non-stick deep-dish pie pan, and bake, using pie weights, until lightly browned, 7 to 10 minutes. Fill with crawfish mixture, and place top crust on pie. Roll up the bottom edge of the pie crust over the top pie crust, then crimp the edges to hold the pie together. Bake until browned, 25 to 30 minutes.

 4 PLATE & SERVE

Slice desired portion of pie, then place onto individual plates. ENJOY!

Cajun Seafood Boil

PREP: 10 MIN	TOTAL: 70 MIN	4-6 SERVINGS

What to Buy

Jumbo Shrimp Andouille Sausage Lemons Butter Balsamic Vinegar Soy Sauce Crushed Red Pepper Salt

Crab Legs Shallots Whole Garlic Fresh Parsley Olive Oil Chili Peppers LeKesh Cajun Black Pepper

Ginger Bay Leaves Thyme Serrano Peppers Worcestershire Honey

Pairing Suggestion

Our favorite pairing with this meal is a Mint Julep.

Utensils

- Large Skillet
- Roasting Pan
- Cooking Spoon
- Knife
- Cutting Board

- Pot
- Measuring Spoons
- Measuring Cups
- 1 Oven Bag

Ingredients

- 3 pounds of raw deveined shrimp with tail on
- 4 snow crab clusters
- ½ pound Andouille sausage
- 1 bulb of garlic, peeled and chopped
- 10 chili peppers
- 5 serrano peppers, steamed
- 2 tablespoons olive oil
- 2 tablespoons of fresh parsley or dry
- 1 whole lemon, slices in half
- Lemon zest

- 2 onions chopped
- 3 tablespoons fresh ginger
- 1/2 cup Worcestershire
- 1/2 balsamic vinegar
- 1/2 cup soy sauce
- 2 tablespoon honey (optional)
- 4 sticks butter
- 2 tablespoons LeKesh Cajun seasoning
- 3 bay leaves
- 3 sprigs of thyme
- Salt
- Pepper

Cajun Seafood Boil

 ## PREPARE

Preheat oven to 375 degrees.

Steam chili and serrano peppers. Then add to food processor with the garlic and fresh ginger. Dice the onions and zest the lemon. Place to the side.

 ## BOIL CORN & POTATOES

In the pot, over medium high heat, boil the potatoes & corn on the cob for 25-30 minutes.

In a large skillet add 2 tablespoons olive oil and onions. Sauté until translucent (about 3 minutes). Add pepper/garlic mixture to pan along with Worcestershire, vinegar, bay leaves, thyme, salt, pepper, and lemon zest. Let simmer 5 minutes.

 ## ADD INGREDIENTS TO BAG

Place plastic oven bag inside a large toaster pan. Open bag and add 4 sticks of butter, lemon halves, then pour sauce mixture from skillet into the bag. Add the raw shrimp, crab legs, andouille sausage, corn and potatoes, and the LeKesh Cajun seasoning to the bag. Close bag and steam 30 minutes on 350 degrees. Remove the bay leaves.

 ## PLATE & SERVE

Enjoy out of the steamed bag to preserve heat or place onto individual plates. ENJOY!

Cajun Roasted Brisket
with a Creole Tomato Sauce

PREP: 30 MIN	TOTAL: 6-8 HOURS	4-6 SERVINGS

What to Buy

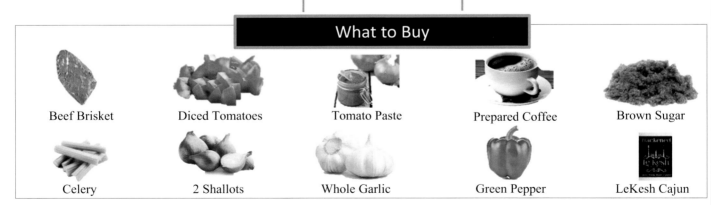

Beef Brisket	Diced Tomatoes	Tomato Paste	Prepared Coffee	Brown Sugar
Celery	2 Shallots	Whole Garlic	Green Pepper	LeKesh Cajun

Pairing Suggestion

Our favorite pairing with this meal is Woodford Reserve Old Fashion.

Utensils

- Roasting Pan

- Cooking Spoon

- Knife

- Cutting Board

- Measuring Spoons

- Measuring Cups

- Mixing Bowl

- 1 Oven Bag

Ingredients

- One 6- to 8-pound beef brisket
- 8 tablespoons of LeKesh Cajun Seasoning
- 2 tablespoons dark brown sugar
- 4 stalks celery, finely chopped
- 8 cloves garlic, minced
- 4 shallots, minced
- 2 green bell peppers, chopped
- One 28-ounce can diced tomatoes with their liquid
- One 6-ounce can tomato paste
- 2 cups of prepared coffee

Cajun Roasted Brisket
with a Creole Tomato Sauce

1 PREPARE

Preheat the oven to 275 degrees.

2 MARINATE THE BRISKET

In a bowl mix LeKesh Cajun Seasoning with the brown sugar. Rub the brisket with the dry seasoned rub, then wrap it tight in plastic. Refrigerator the brisket overnight to seal in the seasoning.

3 ROAST MIXTURE

Opening a large plastic oven bag, Place the brisket in the bag, then in a large toaster oven pan. Top with the celery, garlic, shallots, and green peppers. Pour over the tomatoes and tomato paste and stir, then add the coffee. Cover with foil and bake until the meat is tender and can be shredded easily (about 6-8 hours).

4 BREAKUP THE BRISKET

Using a spatula, breakup the brisket, spreading evenly throughout the bag.

5 PLATE & SERVE

Scoop the mixture onto individual plate. Serve with broccoli and garlic mashed potatoes. ENJOY!

Crab Leg & Shrimp Scampi
with herbed lemon butter sauce

PREP: 10 MIN	TOTAL: 55 MIN	4 SERVINGS

What to Buy

Jumbo Shrimp	1 Box Spaghetti	Lemons	Butter	White Wine	Crushed Red Pepper	Salt
1 LBS Crab Legs	2 Shallots	Whole Garlic	Fresh Parsley	Olive Oil	LeKesh Blackened	Black Pepper

Pairing Suggestion

Our favorite pairing with this meal is an Unoaked Chardonnay.

Utensils

- Large Skillet

- Pot

- Roasting Pan

- Measuring Spoons

- Cooking Spoon

- Measuring Cups

- Knife

- Cheese Grater

- Cutting Board

- 1 Oven Bag

Ingredients

- 2 pounds raw jumbo shrimp, peeled & deveined
- 1 pound snow crab legs
- 1 box spaghetti noodles
- 2 shallots, minced
- 6 cloves of garlic, minced
- 3/4 cup fresh parsley, chopped
- Juice and zest of 2 lemons
- 2 sticks butter
- 8 tablespoons olive oil
- 1 tablespoon crush red pepper
- 1 cup white wine
- 1 tablespoon LeKesh Blackened
- Salt to taste
- Pepper to taste

Crab Leg & Shrimp Scampi
with herbed lemon butter sauce

 PREPARE

Preheat oven to 375 degrees.

Wash and dry all of the vegetables. Next, mince the shallots and garlic cloves, chop the parsley, and zest the lime using the cheese grater. Place each item in a separate bowl or separate on the cutting board in different sections. separate bowl. Lastly, juice the lemon and place in separate bowl. Place all ingredients to the side until needed in the recipe.

 COOK THE VEGGIES

In a large skillet, melt 1 stick of butter . Then add shallots and garlic cooking until translucent. Add the wine and cook until partially absorbed, about 2 minutes. Add the lemon juice, remaining olive oil, the other stick of butter. Heat 3-5 minutes.

 ROAST THE SEAFOOD

Meanwhile, open an oven bag and place it inside of a roasting pan. Add the shrimp, crab legs, and parsley to the bag. Season with LeKesh Blackened, salt, pepper. Pour the butter mixture over the seafood to combine. Squish the contents around until mixture is well incorporated. Bake in the oven for 20-25 minutes.

 BOIL THE PASTA

While seafood is cooking, boil a pot of water, then add spaghetti until el dente (about 10 minutes). Drain the pasta, then rinse it with cold water. Place the pasta to the side.

 PLATE & SERVE

Remove seafood from oven, then pour the spaghetti into the bag to combine with the seafood scampi. ENJOY!

Shrimp & Crab Fried Rice
with Hosin Sauce

PREP: 10 MIN	TOTAL: 50 MIN	4 SERVINGS

What to Buy

Jumbo Shrimp	Jasmine Rice	Ginger	Butter	Corn	Soy Sauce	Hosin Sauce
Crab Legs	Shallots	Whole Garlic	Cilantro	Olive Oil	LeKesh Cajun	Garlic Powder

Pairing Suggestion

Our favorite pairing with this meal is a Moscow Mule.

Utensils

- Large Skillet
- Cooking Spoon
- Knife
- Cutting Board

- Pot
- Measuring Spoons
- Measuring Cups
- Mixing Bowl

Ingredients

- 2 pounds raw jumbo shrimp, peeled & deveined
- 2 cups lump crab
- 1 large shallot
- 6 cloves garlic
- 1/2 inch ginger peeled and minced
- Corn kernels, sliced from 3 boiled corn on the cobs or 1 can of corn
- 2 tablespoons cilantro
- 3/4 cup jasmine rice
- 1 1/4 water
- 6 tablespoons olive oil
- 3 tablespoons butter
- 1 tablespoon LeKesh Cajun or any Cajun seasoning
- 1/4 tablespoon garlic powder
- 2 tablespoons of soy sauce
- 1/4 cup LeKesh Hosin Sauce or store bought

Shrimp & Crab Fried Rice
with Hosin Sauce

 ## 1 PREPARE

Wash and dry all of the vegetables. Next, mince the shallots and garlic cloves, peel and mince the ginger, and chop the cilantro. Place each of the items into a separate bowl or separate on the cutting board in different sections.

 ## 2 MARINADE THE SHRIMP

Clean and dry the shrimp with a paper towel. In a mixing bowl, combine 1/2 of the garlic and ginger. Then add the shrimp to the bowl with Hosin sauce, salt, and pepper. Allow to marinate for 5 minutes. Place to the side. At this point, if you have fresh crab legs, pull the meat out and place into a bowl. If using lump crab in can, move to the next step.

 ## 3 BOIL THE RICE

In a pot, melt 1 tablespoon of butter with the other 1/2 of the ginger. Then add the rice, water, and a pinch of salt. Bring to a boil and reduce heat to low to simmer for 15-18 minutes with the lid on. Clean the same skillet. Add 2 tablespoons of butter, corn, and Cajun seasoning. Add the remainder of the shallots and the garlic. Sauté for 3 minutes, then add in cooked rice and combine well. Add the soy sauce, garlic powder, and cilantro.

 ## 4 COOK THE SHRIMP

In a large skillet or wok, heat 2 tablespoon of olive oil then add the shrimp and cook on each side undisturbed for 3 minutes. Add the crab on top of the shrimp, steaming another minute. Then move to a plate.

 ## 5 PLATE & SERVE

On a large serving plate, pour the cooked rice, then top with the shrimp and crab. Serve extra Hosin sauce to the side. ENJOY!

Eggplant Parmesan Tower
with or without Blackened Shrimp

PREP: 10 MIN	TOTAL: 45 MIN	4 SERVINGS

What to Buy

Eggplant	Breadcrumbs	Buttermilk	Parmesan	Butter	Vegetable Oil	Mozzarella	Salt
Jumbo Shrimp	Shallots	Whole Garlic	Bay Leaf	Fresh Basil	Olive Oil	Marinara	LeKesh Cajun

Pairing Suggestion

Our favorite pairing with this meal is White Zinfandel.

Utensils

- 2 Large Skillets
- Measuring Spoons
- 2 Mixing Bowls
- Measuring Cups
- Cooking Spoon
- Cutting Board
- Knife
- Ovenproof pan

Ingredients

- 1 pound raw shrimp (optional)
- 1 eggplant (sliced into medium steaks)
- Buttermilk
- 1 cup breadcrumbs
- 1 cup fresh parmesan, shredded
- 1 1/2 cup mozzarella, shredded
- 2 cups Newman's Marinara Sauce
- 2 tablespoons butter
- 4 garlic cloves, minced
- 1 shallot, minced
- 1 bay leaf
- Fresh basil, chopped
- 2 tablespoons LeKesh Cajun
- Salt
- 2 cups vegetable oil
- 2 tablespoons olive oil

Eggplant Parmesan Tower
with or without Blackened Shrimp

1 PREPARE

Preheat oven to Broil.

Wash and dry all of the vegetables. Next, mince the shallots and garlic cloves, and chop the basil. Place each item into a separate bowl or separate on the cutting board in different sections.

2 CUT & SOAK THE EGGPLANT

Slice the eggplant into 1 inch steaks width-wise. In one bowl, pour the buttermilk. In the other bowl pour the breadcrumbs and blend with LeKesh Cajun seasoning. Dip, then soak each eggplant into the buttermilk ensuring fully covered, then dip each slice into the breadcrumbs- ensuring that they are fully battered. Place eggplant steaks to the side.

3 COOK SAUCE

In one of the skillets, heat the butter, then add the shallots and garlic (sauté the shrimp at this point if using). Add the marinara, salt, and bay leaf to the skillet and simmer turning the heat to low. Remove the bay leaf.

4 FRY THE EGGPLANT

In the other skillet, heat the vegetable oil on medium to medium high heat until oil becomes hot enough to fry. Fry the eggplant until golden crisp. Place each steak into the ovenproof pan, cover, with marinara, then top with mozzarella and parmesan cheese. Place under broiler for 5 minutes until cheese is melted.

5 PLATE & SERVE

Divide the eggplant parmesan onto individual plates. ENJOY!

Salmon & Shrimp Oven Baked Stew

PREP: 5 MIN	TOTAL: 6 HOURS	4 SERVINGS

What to Buy

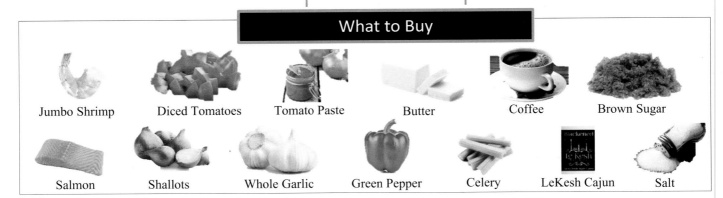

Jumbo Shrimp • Diced Tomatoes • Tomato Paste • Butter • Coffee • Brown Sugar

Salmon • Shallots • Whole Garlic • Green Pepper • Celery • LeKesh Cajun • Salt

Pairing Suggestion

Our favorite pairing with this meal is a Creole Bloody Mary.

Utensils

- Large Skillet

- Roasting Pan

- Cooking Spoon

- Knife

- Cutting Board

- Mixing Bowl

- Measuring Spoons

- Measuring Cups

- 2 Oven Bags

Ingredients

- 1 filet salmon
- 1 pound raw shrimp, deveined
- 8 tablespoons of LeKesh Cajun Seasoning
- 2 tablespoons dark brown sugar
- 1 stick butter
- 4 stalks celery, finely chopped
- 8 cloves garlic, minced
- 4 shallots, chopped
- 2 green bell peppers, chopped
- One 28-ounce can diced tomatoes with their liquid
- One 6-ounce can tomato paste
- 2 cups of prepared coffee
- Salt

Salmon & Shrimp Oven Baked Stew

1 PREPARE
Preheat the oven to 275 degrees F.

2 RUB THE SALMON
In one of the oven bags, add LeKesh Cajun Seasoning and stir in the brown sugar. Rub the salmon and shrimp with the dry rub and refrigerate overnight.

3 ROAST THE VEGETABLES
Opening another oven bag, fill with the celery, garlic, shallots, butter, and green peppers. Pour in the tomatoes and tomato paste and stir, then add the coffee. Close the bag and bake the vegetables for 1 hour.

4 ADD THE SEAFOOD
Remove the pan from the oven. Open the bag, then place the salmon, shrimp, and a pinch of salt in the bag and close. Bake another 30 minutes.

5 PLATE & SERVE
Spoon the stew into individual bowls, then service with cheese rice or garlic mashed potatoes to the side. ENJOY!

Jamaican Curry Shrimp

PREP: 10 MIN	TOTAL: 45 MIN	4 SERVINGS

What to Buy

Jumbo Shrimp — Tomatoes — Green Pepper — Butter — Green Onions — Cornstarch — Salt

Jamaican Curry Powder — Onions — Whole Garlic — Water — Scotch Bonnet Pepper — Black Pepper

Pairing Suggestion

Our favorite pairing with this meal is a Vodka and Ting Martini.

Utensils

- Large Skillet

- Mixing Bowl

- Cooking Spoon

- Knife

- Measuring Spoons

- Measuring Cups

- Cutting Board

Ingredients

- 2 pounds raw shrimp, peeled and deveined

- 2 tablespoons butter

- 2 tablespoons Jamaican curry powder

- 1 tablespoon cornstarch

- 1 scotch bonnet pepper or habanero pepper chopped finely (optional since extremely hot or sub with jalapeño)

- 4 cloves garlic, minced

- 1 onion, diced

- 1/4 green pepper, diced

- 1 tomato, diced

- 2 stalks green onion diced

- Black pepper

- Salt

- 1/2 cup water

Jamaican Curry Shrimp

 PREPARE

Wash and dry all of the vegetables. Next, dice the onion, tomato, green pepper, green onion, mince garlic cloves, and chop the scotch bonnet peppers (optional); placing each in a separate bowl or separate on the chopping board in different sections. Place all ingredients to the side until needed in the recipe.

 MARINADE THE SHRIMP

In a mixing bowl combine the shrimp with 1 tablespoon of curry, then place it to the side for later use.

 SAUTE THE VEGGIES

In a skillet over medium heat, add the butter and 1 tablespoon of curry stirring into a paste as the butter melts. Add the onions, bell pepper, tomato, garlic, green onions, scotch bonnet peppers, and garlic to the skillet and sauté until translucent (about 5 minutes).

 ADD THE SHRIMP

Add the raw shrimp to the vegetable mixture and let sit for about 3-4 minutes then begin to incorporate by stirring the mixture. Add the water, salt, and pepper to the mixture and allow to simmer 5 minutes.

 PLATE & SERVE

Pour mixture into your desire bowl or plates. Serve with Jamaican Rice & Peas and Steamed Cabbage. ENJOY!

Curry Shrimp Tacos
with Mango Habanero Slaw

PREP: 10 MIN	TOTAL: 45 MIN	4 SERVINGS

What to Buy

Jumbo Shrimp	Mango	Lime	Honey	Butter	Tortillas	Cornstarch	Salt

Jamaican Curry Powder	Red Onions	Cilantro	Water	Olive Oil	Green Cabbage	Habanero	Black Pepper

Pairing Suggestion

Our favorite pairing with this meal is Jamaican Rum Punch.

Utensils

- Large Skillet
- 2 Mixing Bowls
- Cooking Spoon
- Knife

- Measuring Spoons
- Measuring Cups
- Cutting Board
- Whisk

Ingredients

- 2 pounds raw shrimp, peeled and deveined
- 2 tablespoons butter
- 2 tablespoons Jamaican curry powder
- 1 tablespoon cornstarch
- Black pepper to taste
- Salt to taste
- 1/2 cup water
- Corn tortilla
- 2 tablespoons honey
- 2 tablespoons lime juice
- 1 tablespoons. olive oil
- 1/2 head green cabbage, thinly shredded
- 2 mangoes, diced
- 1 red onion, thinly sliced
- 2-6 habanero peppers seeded & thinly sliced
- 1/4 cup cilantro chopped

Curry Shrimp Tacos
with Mango Habanero Slaw

 ### PREPARE

Shred the cabbage, slice the red onions and habanero thinly, chop the cilantro, and dice the mango. Place to the side.

In a bowl, whisk the honey, lime juice, and olive oil. Toss the rest of the slaw ingredients in the honey lime sauce. Let the slaw soften while you prepare the shrimp, at least 30 minutes, or overnight

 ### MARINADE THE SHRIMP

In a mixing bowl, combine the shrimp with 1 tablespoon of curry, salt, and pepper. Then place it to the side for later use.

 ### SAUTE THE SHRIMP

Add 1 tablespoon of olive oil, then the shrimp to a skillet over medium heat and cook for about 3 minutes on each side or until pink in color.

 ### STEAM THE TACO SHELLS

Dampen 2 paper towels and place the corn tortillas between them. Microwave the tortillas for 20-30 seconds.

 ### PLATE & SERVE

On individual plates, place desired number of tortilla shells, top with Curry Shrimp, then top with Mango Habanero Slaw. Enjoy!

Blackened Salmon
with Cajun Remoulade

PREP: 5 MIN	TOTAL: 45 MIN	4 SERVINGS

What to Buy

Salmon — Cherry Tomatoes — Butter — Louisiana Hot Sauce — Whole Grain Mustard

Whole Garlic — Olive Oil — LeKesh Blackened — Mayonnaise — LeKesh Cajun

Pairing Suggestion

Our favorite pairing with this meal is a Lemon Drop Martini.

Utensils

- Large Skillet

- Roasting Pan

- Cooking Spoon

- Knife

- Cutting Board

- Mixing Bowl

- Measuring Spoons

- Measuring Cups

Ingredients

For the Salmon:

- 2- 4 oz. salmon fillets
- 2 tablespoons of butter
- 2 tablespoons of olive oil
- 1/2 tablespoon garlic, minced
- 2 tablespoons LeKesh Blackened Seasoning
- Sautéed cherry tomatoes for garnish

Remoulade:

- 1/2 cup mayo
- 2 tablespoon Louisiana hot sauce
- 1/2 tablespoon LeKesh Cajun Seasoning
- 1 tablespoon of whole grain or spicy brown mustard

Blackened Salmon
with Cajun Remoulade

 1 PREPARE

Preheat Oven to 375.

In a separate bowl blend all of the remoulade ingredients until smooth. Place the bowl to the side.

 2 SEASON THE SALMON

Rinse the salmon, then pat dry with a paper towel.

Liberally season each filet with LeKesh Blackened seasoning to your preferred spice level.

 3 SEAR THE SALMON

Heat the large skillet over medium-high heat and add the butter and olive oil. Once the butter has melted, add the salmon and cook about 4 minutes on one side undisturbed. Then flip over using the spatula and cook for another 4 minutes.

 4 BAKE THE SALMON

Place the salmon in the oven an additional 10 minutes for medium or 15-20 minutes for medium-well to well done in temperature.

 5 PLATE & SERVE

Meanwhile, place 2 tablespoons of the remoulade on the center of each plate. Remove the salmon from the oven and place it over the remoulade on each individual plate. Top with sautéed cherry tomatoes for garnish. ENJOY!

Jamaican Rasta Pasta
with Salmon

PREP: 10 MIN	TOTAL: 25 MIN	3-4 SERVINGS

What to Buy

Salmon 1 Box Spaghetti Green Pepper Red Pepper Butter Parmesan Jerk Crushed Red Pepper Salt

Heavy Whipping Cream Yellow Onions Whole Garlic Fresh Parsley Bay Leaves Olive Oil LeKesh Blackened Black Pepper

Pairing Suggestion

Our favorite pairing with this meal is a Moscow Mule.

Utensils

- 2 Large Skillets
- Cooking Spoon
- Knife
- Cutting Board
- Pot
- Measuring Spoons
- Measuring Cups
- Whisk

Ingredients

- 8 oz. or 1/2 filet of salmon
- 16 oz. penne pasta or spaghetti
- 4 tablespoons of homemade marinade/jerk sauce, divided
- 2 tablespoons olive oil, divided
- 1 yellow onion, diced
- 1 green bell pepper, sliced
- 1 red bell pepper, sliced
- 4 garlic cloves, minced
- 2 bay leaves
- 1 stick of butter
- 1 pint heavy cream
- 2 cup grated parmesan, plus more for garnish
- 3 stalks of sliced green onions for garnish (optional)
- LeKesh Blackened seasoning
- crushed red pepper
- salt
- pepper

Jamaican Rasta Pasta
with Salmon

 1 PREPARE

Wash and dry all of the vegetables. Next, dice the onions, mince garlic cloves, and slice the green and red peppers.

Cook pasta according to package instructions to al dente. Drain and set aside.

 2 SEAR THE SALMON

Season salmon with 1 tablespoon of LeKesh Blackened seasoning. In a large skillet over medium heat, heat 1 tablespoon of olive oil. Cook salmon on each side disturbed for 4-5 minutes until lightly charred then add the jerk sauce. Remove from pan and set aside to rest.

 3 COOK THE VEGETABLES

In another skillet, Add remaining oil and cook peppers and onions until mostly tender, 3 to 4 minutes. Add garlic and cook until fragrant, about 1 minute.

Add butter until melted then whisk in Parmesan until fully incorporated and thickened. Add bay leaf, 1 tablespoon of LeKesh Blackened seasoning, and remaining jerk seasoning 2 tablespoons. Add salt & pepper to taste.

 4 COMBINE THE MIXTURE

Add pasta and salmon and toss until completely combined. Remove bay leaves.

5 PLATE & SERVE

Garnish with green onions (optional) and remaining parmesan. Spoon onto individual plates. ENJOY!

Crab Stuffed Salmon

PREP: 15 MIN	TOTAL: 50 MIN	4 SERVINGS

What to Buy

Salmon   Breadcrumbs   Lemons   Butter   Mayonnaise   Mustard   Worcestershire   Salt

Lump Crab Meat   Shallots   Whole Garlic   Fresh Parsley   Olive Oil   Eggs   LeKesh Blackened   Black Pepper

Pairing Suggestion

Our favorite pairing with this meal is Pinot Grigio.

Utensils

- Large Skillet

- Roasting Pan

- Cooking Spoon

- Knife

- Cutting Board

- 2 Mixing Bowls

- Measuring Spoons

- Measuring Cups

- Whisk

- Zest

Ingredients

- 1 filet salmon, cut into 4oz pieces
- 1 pound jumbo lump crabmeat, fresh or pasteurized
- 1 large egg
- 1/4 cup mayonnaise
- 1 tablespoon Dijon mustard
- 3 tablespoon LeKesh Blackened Seasoning
- 1 tablespoon fresh lemon juice
- 1/4 teaspoon of lemon zest
- 1 shallot minced
- 2 garlic cloves minced
- 1 teaspoon Worcestershire sauce
- 1/4 teaspoon salt
- 1 1/2 cups breadcrumbs
- 1 tablespoon fresh parsley chopped
- 2 tablespoon unsalted butter
- 1 tablespoon olive oil
- Lemon wedges for serving

Crab Stuffed Salmon

1 PREPARE

Preheat the oven to 375. Wash and dry all of the vegetables. Next, mince the shallots and garlic cloves, zest (using cheese grater) and juice the lemon, and chop the parsley.

Put the crab in a medium mixing bowl and set aside.. Drain the crabmeat, if necessary, and pick through it for shells (jumbo lump will not have shells).

2 MIX THE STUFFING

In a small bowl, whisk together the egg, mayonnaise, mustard, garlic, shallots, 1 tablespoon LeKesh Blackened Seasoning, lemon juice, lemon zest, Worcestershire sauce, and salt. Fold the mixture over the crab and combine gently. Trying not to turn mixture into a mash. Pour the breadcrumbs and the parsley over the mixture; it should still be fairly loose.

3 STUFF THE SALMON

Liberally season each filet with the remaining LeKesh Blackened seasoning to your preferred spice level. Holding the salmon, cut a pouch for the crabmeat to sit in by using a knife to vertically cut a slit down the middle leaving about an inch on each end of the salmon. Spoon the crab mixture into the salmon pouch you created.

4 BAKE

Spread the olive oil and butter at the bottom of a baking pan. Add the crab stuffed salmon to the pan, then bake for 25-30 minutes. Remove from oven.

5 PLATE & SERVE

Place onto individual plates and garnish with lemon. Serve with your favorite side dish. ENJOY!

Southwest Salmon & Roasted Sweet Potatoes
with Creamy Salsa Verde

PREP: 10 MIN	TOTAL: 45 MIN	2 SERVINGS

What to Buy

Salmon	Roma Tomatoes	Sweet Potatoes	Butter	Jalapenos	Limes	Salt
Red Onions	White Onions	Whole Garlic	Fresh Cilantro	Olive Oil	LeKesh Mexican	Black Pepper

Pairing Suggestion

Our favorite pairing with this meal is a Cosmopolitan Martini.

Utensils

- Large Skillet

- Roasting Pan

- Cooking Spoon

- Knife

- Cutting Board

- Mixing Bowl

- Measuring Spoons

- Measuring Cups

- Cheese Grater

Ingredients

- 2-4 oz. salmon fillets
- 2 sweet potatoes, diced small
- 2 roma tomatoes, diced
- 1 red onion, diced
- 2 tablespoon of minced white onions
- Juice and zest of 1 lime (separated)
- 2 tablespoons of cilantro, minced
- 2 cloves of garlic, minced
- 1 jalapeño or serrano, minced
- 1 jalapeño or serrano, diced
- 4 tablespoons olive oil
- 4 tablespoons of sour cream
- 3 tablespoons of LeKesh Mexican
- Salt
- Pepper
- Creamy salsa verde, page 80

Southwest Salmon & Roasted Sweet Potatoes
with Creamy Salsa Verde

 PREPARE

Preheat oven to 425 degrees. Wash and dry all of the vegetables. Next, mince the shallots and garlic cloves, peel and mince the ginger, chop the cilantro, and zest then juice the lime. Next, dice the poblano, sweet potatoes, and red onions. Place each item in a separate bowl or separate on the cutting board in different sections.

 ROAST THE VEGETABLES

Take out the roasting pan and drizzle 1 tablespoon of olive oil, then place diced sweet potatoes, red onions, and poblano peppers onto the pan. Season with 2 tablespoon of LeKesh Mexican, salt, and pepper, then drizzle with olive oil. Bake 25 minutes.

 COOK THE BAKE SALMON

In a skillet, heat 1 tablespoon of olive oil. Season salmon with 1 tablespoon of LeKesh Mexican, salt, and pepper, then place into the hot skillet. Cook 5 minutes on each side undisturbed. If medium-well to well done is desired, place in oven for an additional 7-10 minutes. Place cooked salmon to the side.

 COMBINE THE MIXTURE

In a separate bowl, combine the diced tomatoes and the zest of lime. Remove poblano mixture from oven and mix in tomato/lime zest..

 PLATE & SERVE

Spoon the sweet potato mixture onto the side of a plate. Place the salmon to the center of plate, then spoon creamy salsa verde (page 80) over entire meal. Garnish with sliced jalapeños. ENJOY!

Salmon Croquette Stuffed Biscuits

PREP: 10 MIN	TOTAL: 55 MIN	4 SERVINGS

What to Buy

Pink Salmon   Green Pepper   Celery   Milk   Butter   Worcestershire   Grain Mustard   Hot Sauce

Jumbo Can Biscuits   Yellow Onions   Whole Garlic   Olive Oil   Mayonnaise   Capers   LeKesh Blackened   Black Pepper

Gouda Slices   Onion Powder   Garlic Powder   Breadcrumbs   Egg   Fresh Oregano   Basil   Parsley

Pairing Suggestion

Our favorite pairing with this meal is a Cognac Pineapple Margarita.

Utensils

- Large Skillet
- Roasting Pan
- Cooking Spoon
- Knife
- Whisk

- Measuring Spoons
- Measuring Cups
- Cutting Board
- Mixing Bowl
- Rolling Pin

Ingredients

Salmon Croquette Ingredients:

- Canned pink salmon
- 1/2 cup bell pepper
- 1/2 cup onion
- 1/4 cup celery
- 2 eggs
- 1/4 cup milk
- 1 teaspoon fresh basil
- 1 teaspoon fresh oregano

- Grain mustard
- 2 garlic cloves, chopped
- Onion powder
- Garlic powder
- Black pepper
- LeKesh Blackened Seasoning
- 1/2 Italian breadcrumbs
- Worcestershire
- Jumbo biscuits (8)
- Gouda cheese slices (8)

Garlic Butter Topping:

- 1/2 stick butter
- 1 teaspoon garlic powder
- 1/2 teaspoon onion powder
- 1 teaspoon parsley
- Grated parmesan

Remoulade:

- 1 tablespoon LeKesh Blackened Seasoning
- 1 tablespoon mayo
- 1 teaspoon grain mustard
- 1 tablespoon hot sauce
- 1 teaspoon capers

Salmon Croquette Stuffed Biscuits

1 PREPARE

Preheat oven to 350 degrees. Wash and dry all of the vegetables. Next, chop the onions, celery, and green peppers. Mince garlic cloves, basil, oregano, and parsley. Place each item into a separate bowl or separate on the cutting board in different sections.

2 MAKE CROQUETTE BALLS

In a mixing bowl, scramble the 2 eggs, then pour in the milk and whisk together. Toss in the onions, bell pepper, celery, basil, oregano, and seasonings, then whisk until fully combined. Fold in the salmon combining with your hands ensure not to over crumble. Pour in the Worcestershire then the breadcrumbs and continue to fold until fully combined. Using a 1/4 cup measuring cup, scoop out salmon mixture and form 8 balls.

3 PAN FRY THE CROQUETTES

Heat skillet over medium heat with 2 cups of oil fully coating the bottom of the pan about 1/2 inch. Once oil is heated scoop 1/4 cup of salmon croquette mixture into the oil. Cook each side about 3 minutes until golden. Place completed croquette balls onto a plate lined with paper towel to absorb oil.

4 STUFF THE BISCUITS

Meanwhile, open your can of biscuits, place onto a cutting board and roll with pin until flat. Once each biscuit is flat, place the Gouda cheese on top of each one. Place a salmon ball on top of each biscuit. Fold the biscuit around the ball until fully enclosed.

5 BAKE THE BALLS

Place balls into glass pan ensuring that the sides are touching. Bake for 15 minutes or until biscuits are golden.

6 PLATE & SERVE

For the garlic butter: Put the butter into a small glass bowl with the garlic powder, onion powder, parsley and microwave for 45 seconds or until fully melted. Stir to combine. Remove biscuits from oven and spoon or brush the garlic butter over the biscuits. Sprinkle freely with parmesan to your liking.

For the remoulade: Whisk all the Ingredients together. Place on individual plates, and serve with remoulade. ENJOY!

Catfish, Shrimp & Elote Grits

| PREP: 10 MIN | TOTAL: 60 MIN | 4 -6 SERVINGS |

What to Buy

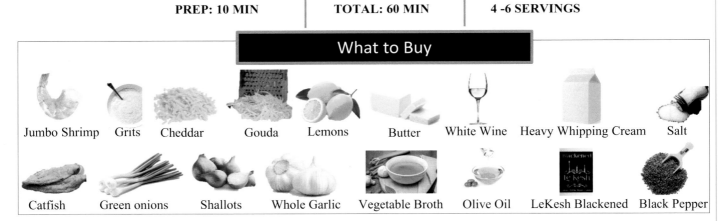

Jumbo Shrimp   Grits   Cheddar   Gouda   Lemons   Butter   White Wine   Heavy Whipping Cream   Salt

Catfish   Green onions   Shallots   Whole Garlic   Vegetable Broth   Olive Oil   LeKesh Blackened   Black Pepper

Pairing Suggestion

Our favorite pairing with this meal is a Lemon Basil Vodka Martini.

Utensils

- Large Skillet

- Mixing Bowl

- Cooking Spoon

- Knife

- Cutting Board

- Pot

- Measuring Spoons

- Measuring Cups

- Whisk

Ingredients

- 1 cup grits to 4 cups water (4 servings prepared based on package)
- 2 pounds raw jumbo shrimp, peeled & deveined
- 12 catfish nuggets fried
- 2 shallots, minced
- 1 head of garlic, minced
- 2 cups green onions, chopped
- 1 stick butter
- 3/4 cup sharp cheddar cheese, shredded

- 1/2 cup grated Parmesan cheese
- 1/2 cup smoked Gouda, shredded
- 1 pint heavy cream
- 2 tablespoons lemon juice
- 3 tablespoons white wine
- 4 tablespoons olive oil
- 1/2 cup vegetable broth
- 2 tablespoons LeKesh Cajun Seasoning
- Salt/pepper to taste

Catfish, Shrimp & Elote Grits

1 PREPARE

Wash and dry all of the vegetables. Next, mince the onions, shallots and garlic, chop the green onions, and juice the lemon. Place each item in a separate bowl or separate on the cutting board in different sections.

2 MAKE THE CREAM SAUCE

In a large skillet, melt the butter, then add the shallots and garlic sautéing 2-3 minutes, then add the white wine and lemon juice, cook another minute. Slowly whisk in the cheeses until melted. Slowly whisk in the heavy whipping cream. Add salt and pepper to taste. Add 1/2 cup vegetable broth if mixture appears too thick. Reduce heat to low and simmer.

3 COOK SHRIMP & CATFISH

Fry the catfish to your liking and place on a paper menu lined plate. Season shrimp with LeKesh Cajun seasoning. In a medium skillet, heat 2 tablespoons of olive oil then add shrimp and cook 3 minutes undisturbed on each side. Remove shrimp and place to the side.

4 BOIL THE GRITS

In a large pot with lid, cook grits according to package. Whisk in grits, then whisk again after about 3 minutes. Remove grits from heat.

5 COMBINE THE MIXTURE

Stir the cream sauce into the grit mixture until smooth. Return grits to the stove on low heat. Add the green onions to the pot. Remove from heat.

6 PLATE & SERVE

Scoop the cheese grits onto a plate or bowl. Then top with 1/4 cup of Elote, a generous portion of Cajun shrimp and 3 catfish nuggets. * See Mexican Corn Elote recipe (page 19).

Jerk Salmon Fajitas

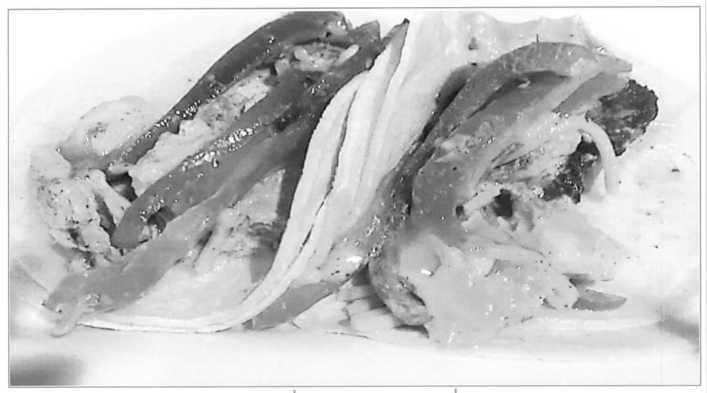

PREP: 10 MIN	TOTAL: 45 MIN	2-4 SERVINGS

What to Buy

Salmon	Yellow Onions	Limes	Corn Tortillas	Jerk Sauce	Scotch Bonnet Sauce
Mexican Cheese	Green Peppers	Red Peppers	Fresh Cilantro	Olive Oil	LeKesh Mexican

Pairing Suggestion

Our favorite pairing with this meal is a Jamaican Stout Beer.

Utensils

- Large Skillet

- Roasting Pan

- Cooking Spoon

- Knife

- Mixing Bowl

- Measuring Spoons

- Measuring Cups

- Cutting Board

Ingredients

- 2-4 oz. salmon fillets
- 1 red peppers, sliced
- 1 green peppers, sliced
- 1 yellow onion, sliced
- 1 tablespoon fresh cilantro, minced
- LeKesh Mexican Seasoning or store bought
- LeKesh Jerk Sauce or store bought
- 1/2 cup Mexican Cheese
- 8 corn tortillas
- 3 tablespoons olive oil
- Scotch bonnet sauce (optional)
- 1 lime, quartered in slices

Jerk Salmon Fajitas

 1 # PREPARE

Preheat oven to 475.

In a mixing bowl, season the salmon with LeKesh Mexican seasoning or any store bought.

 2 # SAUTE THE VEGETABLES

Heat 1 tablespoon of the olive oil in a skillet to medium heat. Then add the onions, greens pepper, red peppers. Remove from heat, then place the mixture to the side onto a plate.

 3 # SEAR THE SALMON

Add 2 tablespoons of olive oil to the skillet. Then place the salmon in the hot pan and allow to cook 3 minutes on each side undisturbed.

Brush the fillets with Jerk Sauce. Place in the oven pan and into the oven for 15 for medium or 20-25 minutes medium well to well.

 4 # STEAM & FILL THE SHELLS

Wrap the tortillas in a damp paper towel. Place in the microwave for 30-60 seconds, or until warm. Fill each of the tortillas with salmon, peppers, Mexican cheese, and some scotch bonnet pepper sauce (optional)!

 5 # PLATE & SERVE

Place the tacos onto individual plates. Garnish with a lime. ENJOY!

Black Bean & Poblano Enchiladas

with Lime Crema

| PREP: 10 MIN | TOTAL: 40 MIN | 4 SERVINGS |

What to Buy

Black Beans   Green Onions   Roma Tomato   Limes   Mexican Cheese   Flour Tortillas   Sour Cream   Salt

Poblano   Onion   Cilantro   Whole Garlic   Serrano Peppers   Olive Oil   Salsa   LeKesh Mexican   Black Pepper

Pairing Suggestion

Our favorite pairing with this meal is a Paloma Martini.

Utensils

- Large Skillet

- Ovenproof Pan

- Cooking Spoon

- Knife

- Cheese Grater

- 2 Mixing Bowls

- Measuring Spoons

- Measuring Cups

- Cutting Board

Ingredients

- 1 can of refried black beans
- 1 poblano pepper
- 4 green onion stalks (white separates from greens)
- 1 small onion diced
- 3 tablespoons fresh cilantro, chopped
- 2 garlic cloves, minced
- 2 tablespoons plus ¼ teaspoon LeKesh Mexican
- Roma tomatoes
- 2 tablespoons olive oil
- 6 flour tortillas
- 1 cup Mexican Cheese
- I serrano pepper
- 1 jar salsa
- 1 cup Sour Cream
- Juice and zest of 1 Lime
- Salt
- Pepper

Black Bean & Poblano Enchiladas
with Lime Crema

1 PREPARE

Preheat the oven to 375.

Wash and dry all of the vegetables. Next, dice the poblano and onions, chop the cilantro and green onions. mince garlic cloves, and zest and juice the lime. Place to the side.

2 SAUTE THE VEGGIES

In a skillet over medium heat, drizzle olive oil. Then add poblano peppers, onions, and garlic until softened (about 3-4 minutes). Add 2 tablespoons LeKesh Mexican, salt, the tomatoes, and the whites of the green onions. Cook the mixture 5 more minutes.

3 FILL, ROLL, & BAKE

Spread 1 tablespoon of the refried black beans and cilantro onto each tortilla, then scoop even amounts of the poblano mixture onto each tortilla. Roll the tortillas from the filled side with the seam placed down. Place the tortillas in an ovenproof pan ensuring that the tortillas are touch each other. Next, Spoon salsa over the tortillas spreading enough to cover and coat each one. Sprinkle the Mexican cheese over the enchiladas. Bake until the cheese is melted about 5 minutes.

4 MAKE THE CREMA

In a small mixing bowl, add sour cream, 1/4 teaspoon of LeKesh Mexican, zest of the lime, and squeeze the juice of the lime. Season with salt and pepper then stir.

5 PLATE & SERVE

Remove the enchiladas from the oven, then top them with lime crema drizzles, the greens of the green onions, and as much chopped Serrano peppers as you prefer. ENJOY!

Let's "Mardi Di Gras Parade" to these DESSERTS

For about 10 years, I hosted themed birthday parties that included a well thought-out dinner menu at a contemporary venue to bring the idea to life. The event pictured below was themed, "Mysterious Masquerade". Guests were asked to come masked or one was provided at the door (yet, some didn't keep them on for the photo…smile). Throughout the night, we enjoyed New Orleans Creole style cuisine, played games that included prizes, then danced the night away with a live band. I like to say, I was the innovator of the themed events.

Make time to make memories….with Fun & Laughter!

New Orleans Bread Pudding
with Bourbon Sauce & Cinnamon Cream Frosting

PREP: 10 MIN	TOTAL: 2HOURS, 30 MIN	8 SERVINGS

What to Buy

Loaf French Bread	Brown Sugar	Sugar	Pure Vanilla Extract	Butter	Bourbon	Cornstarch
Eggs	Cinnamon	All-Spice	Heavy Whipping Cream	Half & Half		Raisins

Pairing Suggestion

Our favorite pairing with this meal is a Bourbon Cream Coffee.

Utensils

- Large Skillet

- Loaf Pan

- Cooking Spoon

- Knife

- Cutting Board

- 3 Mixing Bowls

- Measuring Spoons

- Measuring Cups

- Whisk

- Hand Mixer

Ingredients

- 1 tablespoon unsalted butter
- 4 large eggs
- 1 cup brown sugar
- 1/2 teaspoon ground cinnamon
- 1/8 teaspoon freshly grated allspice
- 1 tablespoon pure vanilla extract
- 1/4 cup Bourbon
- 2 cups half-and-half
- 1 loaf day-old French bread, cut into 1-inch cubes (about 6-7 cups)
- 1/2 cup raisins (optional), or more if desired

CINNAMON CREAM FROSTING

- 1 1/4 cups heavy cream
- 1/4 cup granulated sugar
- 1/2 teaspoon ground cinnamon
- 1/8 teaspoon allspice

BOURBON SAUCE

- 1 cup heavy cream
- 1 cup half-and-half
- 2 teaspoons pure vanilla extract
- 6 tablespoons sugar
- 1 tablespoon cornstarch
- 3 tablespoons bourbon

New Orleans Bread Pudding
with Bourbon Sauce & Cinnamon Cream Frosting

1 **PREPARE**

Preheat the oven to 350ºF.

Grease a loaf pan with the butter. Cut the French bread into 1-inch cubes. Set aside.

2 **SOAK THE BREAD**

Whisk the eggs, sugar, cinnamon, allspice, vanilla, and bourbon together in a large mixing bowl. Add the half-and-half and mix well. Add the bread and raisins. Allow the mixture to soak to the side for 2 hours, stirring occasionally.

3 **BAKE THE BREAD**

Pour the mixture into the loaf pan. Bake until set in the center, about 55 minutes. Let bread to cool for 5 minutes before serving.

4 **MIX THE BOURBON SAUCE**

Heat the cream, half-and-half, vanilla, and the sugar in a skillet over high heat; whisking, for 3 minutes. Combine the cornstarch with the bourbon. Whisk the bourbon into the mixture. Turn heat to low and simmer for 1 minute.

5 **CINNAMON CREAM FROSTING**

Blend the cream with a mixer on high speed for about 2 minutes. Add the sugar, cinnamon, and allspice allowing the mixture to thicken to frosting consistency.

6 **PLATE & SERVE**

When ready to serve, spoon the bourbon sauce, then the cinnamon cream frosting over the bread pudding. Enjoy!

Lemon-Lime Overboard Pound Cake

PREP: 10 MIN	TOTAL: 1 HOUR 55 MIN	8-10 SERVINGS

What to Buy

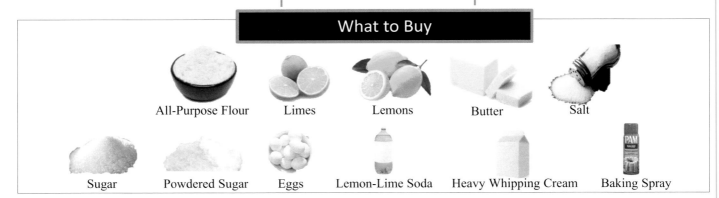

All-Purpose Flour Limes Lemons Butter Salt

Sugar Powdered Sugar Eggs Lemon-Lime Soda Heavy Whipping Cream Baking Spray

Pairing Suggestion

Our favorite pairing with this meal is a Vodka Mojito.

Utensils

- Large Skillet
- Loaf Pan
- Cooking Spoon
- Knife
- Cutting Board
- 2 Mixing bowls
- Measuring Spoons
- Measuring Cups
- Cheese Grater
- Hand Mixer

Ingredients

For the Pound Cake:

- 3 cups sugar
- 3 sticks unsalted butter
- 5 eggs
- 3 cups all-purpose flour
- 1/2 teaspoon salt
- 1 cup lemon-lime soda, such as 7-Up
- 1 tablespoon lemon zest
- 1 tablespoon lime zest
- Nonstick baking spray

For the Frosting/Glaze:

- 2 cups powdered sugar, sifted
- 1 tablespoon lemon zest and juice
- 1 tablespoon lime zest and lime juice
- 1/4 teaspoon salt
- 1 cup heavy cream
- 1 teaspoon granulated sugar

Lemon-Lime Overboard Pound Cake

1 PREPARE

Preheat the oven to 325 degrees. Spray the loaf pan with baking nonstick spray.

Juice and zest a lemon, then separate into individual bowls. Next juice and zest a lime and put into two separate bowls. Set to the side.

2 CREAM THE MIXTURES

Using a mixing bowl and the hand mixer, blend together the sugar and butter. Slow add in the eggs, blending one at a time.

In a separate bowl, combine the flour and salt. Next, add the butter and sugar mixture into the dry mix 1 cup at a time, constantly whisking.

3 FINALIZE THE MIXTURE

Put the hand mixture on low setting, then slowly add the lemon-lime soda and mix until well combined. Next, add the lemon and lime zest and mix well.

Pour the batter into a loaf pan ensuring that the mixture is leveled.

4 BAKE THE POUNDCAKE

Bake for the cake 1 hour and 10 minutes or until a toothpick comes out clean. Remove the cake from the oven. Allow to cool for 15 minutes. Once cooled, turn the cake upside down onto a cake platter or large plate. Allow to cool another 15 minutes while you make the frosting glaze.

5 CREATE THE GLAZE

Combine the powdered sugar, lemon zest and juice, lime zest and juice, salt, and 1 tablespoon water. Whisk until thickened. Drizzle frosting over the pound cake. ENJOY!

Apple Cinnamon Cheesecake
or Cheesecake Ball

| PREP: 10 MIN | TOTAL: 1 HOUR, 25 MIN | 8 SERVINGS |

What to Buy

Green Apples Sugar Lemons Graham Cracker Crust Heavy Whipping Cream

Cinnamon Eggs Pure Vanilla Extract Cream Cheese Butter

Pairing Suggestion

Our favorite pairing with this dessert is an Irish Cream Coffee.

Utensils

- Large Skillet

- 2 Mixing Bowls

- Deep Pie Dish

- Measuring Spoons

- Cooking Spoon

- Measuring Cups

- Knife

- Hand Mixer

- Cutting Board

Ingredients

- 6 green apples
- 4 – 8 oz. cream cheese
- 2 tablespoons heavy whipping cream
- 1 cup sugar, plus 3 tablespoons
- 4 eggs
- 1 tablespoon vanilla extract
- 1 ½ tablespoons cinnamon
- 1 1/2 cups graham cracker crumbs
- 2 sticks butter
- Juice of 1 lemon
- Drizzle of caramel sauce (optional)

Apple Cinnamon Cheesecake
or Cheesecake Balls

1 **PREPARE**

Heat oven to 325°F.

Slice the apples thinly. Place to the side.

2 **CREATE THE FILLING**

In one of the mixing bowls, beat cream cheese, heavy whipping cream, 1 cup sugar, and the vanilla with hand mixer until blended. Add eggs, 1 at a time, mixing on low speed until blended.

3 **SAUTÉ THE APPLES**

In a mixing bowl, combine the apples with ¼ cup brown sugar, 1 tablespoon of cinnamon, and the lemon juice.

Heat the skillet over medium heat with 1 stick of butter and add the apples. Sauté the apples for 3-4 minutes until softened.

4 **BLEND THE CRUST**

Combine graham crumbs, 1/2 tablespoon cinnamon, 3 tablespoons of sugar, 1 stick of melted butter. Once well blended, press graham cracker mixture onto bottom of the pie baking dish.

Pour cream cheese mixture over crust. Add the apple slices on top decorating neatly.

5 **BAKE THE CHEESECAKE**

Bake 55 min. or until center is almost set. Run knife around rim of pan to loosen cake. Refrigerate cheesecake 4 hours.

6 **PLATE & SERVE**

Plate the cheesecake onto individual plates. ENJOY!

Apple Cinnamon Cobbler
(or Peach or Mango Cinnamon Cobbler)

PREP: 10 MIN	TOTAL: 1 HOUR 30 MIN	12 SERVINGS

What to Buy

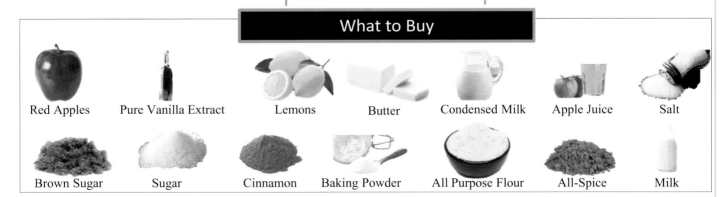

Red Apples Pure Vanilla Extract Lemons Butter Condensed Milk Apple Juice Salt

Brown Sugar Sugar Cinnamon Baking Powder All Purpose Flour All-Spice Milk

Pairing Suggestion

Our favorite pairing with this item is a Prosecco.

Utensils

- 9 x 13 inch pan

- Mixing Bowl

- Cooking Spoon

- Knife

- Cutting Board

- Pot

- Measuring Spoons

- Measuring Cups

- Whisk

Ingredients

For the filling:

- 8 red apples, sliced thinly
- 2 cups apple juice
- 1 cup water
- 1 stick butter
- 1/3 cup brown sugar
- ¼ cup sugar
- Juice of 1 lemon
- 2 tablespoons vanilla extract
- 1 tablespoon cinnamon
- 1/4 teaspoon all spice
- Eagle Brand condensed milk

For the batter:

- 1 cup all-purpose flour
- 1 cup granulated sugar
- 2 teaspoons baking powder
- 1/4 teaspoon salt
- 3/4 cup milk
- 5 tablespoons butter, melted

For the topping:

- 1/4 teaspoon ground cinnamon
- 1/8 teaspoon sugar

Apple Cinnamon Cobbler
(or Peach or Mango Cobbler)

 PREPARE

Preheat the oven to 350 degrees. Slice the apples thinly. (If substituting, for peach, use 2 large cans with the juice and for mango use 12 fresh mangos sliced thinly.

 COOK THE APPLES

In a pot over medium heat, Combine water, apple juice, lemon juice, vanilla extract, and butter. Add apples to the liquid and Boil for 4 minutes. Then add sugar and brown sugar. Cook another 3 minutes, then Mix with a spoon then add condensed milk. Cool 1 minute and remove from heat. Lightly spray a 9 x 13 inch baking dish, then pour mixture into pan.

 PREPARE THE BATTER

In a mixing bowl, pour flour, sugar, baking powder, and salt. Mix dry ingredients together with a whisk. Then gradually add the milk and melted butter. Stir until smooth.

Spoon droplets of the batter over the apple mixture cover majority of the apples.

 BAKE THE COBBLER

Place baking dish in the oven. Bake for 38-40 minutes.

Mix the cinnamon and sugar for topping. 10 minutes before pulling the cobbler out of the oven. Sprinkle with cinnamon sugar topping and allow to bake the final 10 minutes. Remove cobbler from oven and cool for 10 minutes.

PLATE & SERVE

Place cobbler onto individual plates with a scoop of vanilla bean ice cream. ENJOY!

Pass Me the Sauce
MISCELLANEOUS

When my son was born, all of the creative energy from my themed parties and restaurant exploration days transitioned to his birthday parties; along with the finances to sponsor it.

Make time to make memories....with your #1 Fans!

Agave Honey Mustard Salad Dressing

PREP: 5 MIN	TOTAL: 5 MIN	4 SERVINGS

What to Buy

Agave Syrup	Dijon Mustard	Apple Cider Vinegar	Ground Cinnamon	Olive Oil	Fresh Parsley	Salt

Pairing Suggestion

Our favorite pairing with this item is New Zealand Sauvignon Blanc.

Utensils

- Mixing Bowl

- Measuring Spoons

- Mixing Spoon

- Measuring Cups

- Whisk

Ingredients

- 1/4 cup plus 1 tablespoon Dijon mustard

- 1/4 cup agave syrup

- 1/4 cup cider vinegar

- 1 1/2 teaspoons kosher salt

- 1 tablespoon parsley

- 1 teaspoon ground cinnamon

- 1/4 cup plus 2 tablespoons olive oil (may use soy, peanut, or corn)

Agave Honey Mustard Salad Dressing

1 PREPARE

In a medium bowl, whisk together the mustard, agave, vinegar, parsley, cinnamon, and salt. Gradually whisk in the olive oil to make a creamy dressing. Use immediately or store in the refrigerator, covered, for up to 3 days.

2 SERVE

Use on various salads including LeKesh recipe items such as the Waldorf or Jerk Salmon salad.

Mango Habanero Slaw

| PREP: 10 MIN | TOTAL: 40 MIN | 4 SERVINGS |

What to Buy

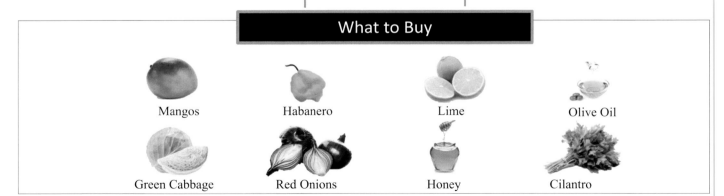

| Mangos | Habanero | Lime | Olive Oil |
| Green Cabbage | Red Onions | Honey | Cilantro |

Pairing Suggestion

Our favorite pairing with this item a Mango Margarita.

Utensils

- Mixing Bowl

- Cooking Spoon

- Knife

- Cutting Board

- Measuring Spoons

- Measuring Cups

- Whisk

Ingredients

- 1/2 head green cabbage thinly shredded
- 2 mangoes diced
- 1 red onion thinly sliced
- 2-6 habanero peppers seeded & thinly sliced
- 2 tablespoons honey
- 2 tablespoons lime juice
- 1 tablespoons. olive oil
- 1/4 cup cilantro chopped

Mango Habanero Slaw

1 PREPARE

Shred the cabbage, red onions, and habanero thinly, chop the cilantro, and dice the mango.

Whisk honey, lime juice, and olive oil in a large bowl.

2 TOSS THE MIXTURE

Toss the rest of the slaw ingredients in the honey lime sauce. Let soften at least 30 minutes, or overnight

3 SERVE

Enjoy on top of tacos, salads, and more!

Creamy Salsa Verde

PREP: 10 MIN	TOTAL: 20 MIN	4 SERVINGS

What to Buy

Sour Cream

Limes

Fresh Cilantro

Jalapenos or Serrano's

Yellow Onions

Whole Garlic

LeKesh Mexican

Pairing Suggestion

Our favorite pairing with this item is a Mint Julep.

Utensils

- Mixing Bowl

- Cooking Spoon

- Knife

- Cutting Board

- Measuring Spoons

- Measuring Cups

- Cheese Grater

Ingredients

- 1 cup sour cream
- Juice of 4 limes
- Zest of 1 lime
- 8 garlic cloves, minced
- 4 jalapeno or serrano peppers, minced
- ½ cup yellow onions, minced
- ½ cup of cilantro, minced
- 1 tablespoon LeKesh Mexican or store bought taco seasoning

Creamy Salsa Verde

1 PREPARE

Zest the lime, juice the lime, mince the garlic, jalapeno, cilantro and onion. Place to the side.

2 COMBINE THE MIXTURE

In a mixing bowl, combine sour cream, juice of lime, garlic, minced jalapeños, white onions, cilantro, and LeKesh Mexican seasoning. Mix until combined. Place in the refrigerator while preparing remaining items.

3 SERVE

Use on various LeKesh recipes or on a variety of Mexican dishes.

Homemade Guacamole

PREP: 10 MIN	TOTAL: 20 MIN	4 SERVINGS

What to Buy

Avocados

Limes

Jalapenos or Serrano's

Yellow Onions

Whole Garlic

Fresh Cilantro

LeKesh Mexican

Pairing Suggestion

Our favorite pairing with this meal is a Traditional Lime Margarita.

Utensils

- Mixing Bowl
- Cooking Spoon
- Knife
- Cutting Board
- Measuring Spoons
- Cheese Grater

Ingredients

- 3 Avocadoes
- ½ yellow onion, minced
- 1 jalapeno or serrano, minced
- 4 garlic cloves, minced
- 2 tablespoons fresh cilantro, minced
- Juice and zest of 1 Lime
- 1 tablespoon LeKesh Mexican Seasoning or store-bought

Homemade Guacamole

 1 PREPARE

Zest the lime, juice the lime, mince the garlic, jalapeno or serrano, cilantro, and onion. Place in the mixing bowl.

 2 SLICE THE AVOCADO

Slice the avocado in half lengthwise, then discard the seed and scoop out the avocado flesh.

 3 COMBINE MIXTURE

Combine the avocado in the bowl with the vegetable mixture mashing with a fork or potato masher. Add in LeKesh Mexican Seasoning. Then, use your spoon to blend the mixture together until smooth.

 4 PLATE & SERVE

Place into serving bowl. Serve with tortilla chips or on your favorite Mexican dish. ENJOY!

Jamaican Jerk Sauce

PREP: 25 MIN	TOTAL: 25 MIN	4 SERVINGS

What to Buy

Scotch Bonnet Peppers	All Spice	Sugar	Nutmeg	Limes	Soy Sauce	Orange Juice	Salt

Fresh Ginger	White Onions	Whole Garlic	Fresh Thyme	Olive Oil	White Vinegar	Black Pepper

Pairing Suggestion

Our favorite pairing with this item is a Rum Punch.

Utensils

- Cooking Spoon
- Knife
- Cutting Board
- Measuring Spoons
- Measuring Cups
- Blender

Ingredients

- 6 sliced scotch bonnet peppers or jalapenos
- 1 whole bulb of garlic, finely chopped
- 3 white onions, finely chopped
- 1 tablespoon fresh ginger, peeled and chopped
- 2 tablespoon fresh thyme
- 2 tablespoon ground allspice
- 2 tablespoon sugar
- 2 tablespoon salt
- 2 teaspoons nutmeg
- 2 tablespoon ground black pepper
- 1/2 cup olive oil
- 1/2 cup soy sauce
- Juice of one lime
- 1 cup orange juice
- 1 cup white vinegar

Jamaican Jerk Sauce

 PREPARE

Slice the peppers, chop the garlic, onions, and ginger.

 BLEND INGREDIENTS

Mix all the ingredients together in a blender until mixture is well combined as a liquid.

 SERVE

Enjoy as a sauce on jerk chicken, fish, shrimp, and many more!

Remoulade Sauce

PREP: 5 MIN	TOTAL: 5 MIN	2 SERVINGS

What to Buy

Mayonnaise	Capers	Grain Mustard	Hot Sauce	LeKesh Blackened

Pairing Suggestion

Our favorite pairing with this item is a Hurricane.

Utensils

- Mixing Bowl

- Measuring Spoons

- Mixing Spoon

- Whisk

Ingredients

- 1 tablespoon LeKesh Blackened Seasoning
- 1 tablespoon mayo
- 1 teaspoon grain mustard
- 1 tablespoon hot sauce
- 1 teaspoon capers, minced

Remoulade Sauce

1 PREPARE

In a mixing bowl, whisk all the Ingredients together until well blended.

2 SERVE

Use on Seafood Po-Boys, LeKesh Salmon Croquette Stuffed Biscuits or Blackened Salmon. Enjoy!

Hosin Sauce

PREP: 10 MIN	TOTAL: 10 MIN	2 SERVINGS

What to Buy

Soy Sauce   Peanut Butter   Sirachi Sauce   Black Pepper

Rice Vinegar   Honey   Whole Garlic   Olive Oil

Pairing Suggestion

Our favorite pairing with this item is an Elderflower Sake Martini.

Utensils

- Mixing Bowl

- Measuring Spoons

- Mixing Spoon

Ingredients

- 4 tablespoons soy sauce
- 2 tablespoons peanut butter
- 1 tablespoon honey
- 2 teaspoons rice vinegar
- 1 garlic clove minced
- 2 teaspoons olive oil
- 1 teaspoon sirachi sauce
- 1/8 teaspoon black pepper

Hosin Sauce

1 PREPARE

In a mixing bowl, combine all ingredients and whisk until well blended.

2 SERVE

Enjoy on various rice dishes such as LeKesh Crab Leg & Shrimp Fried Rice.